Reckless

C. E. Zachary

Reckless Copyright © 2012 by C.E. Zachary

All rights reserved.

DREAM WRITE NOW

www.DreamWriteNow.com

Printed in the United States of America. The contents of this book are the sole original creations of its author and are protected under US Copyright laws. No part of this book may be reproduced, stored in or introduced into a retrieval system, or transmitted in any from, by any means (electronical, mechanical, photocopy, recording, or otherwise) without the expressed written consent of the copyright owner.

ISBN-13 978-1477620649

Photography by V. Pelt

Cover Design by Corinne Forrester www.lucidbird.com

Edited by Saleem Clarke

First Edition

Thanks

To the women in my life who made me who I am today: my Mother, Nana, Grandmother, Aunt Harriet, Aunt Susan, Aunt Nancy, Aunt Patrice, Cousin Barbara, Cousin Maria, Cousin Jessica, and Cousin Heather, Margie, Lauren, Linda, Ceyda, Lauren, Shaneen and every other woman who has touched my life in some way.

A special word for my Nana, who believed all women, no matter how old, should wear their beauty out in public with pride. Your beautiful, womanly spirit lives with us forever and ever.

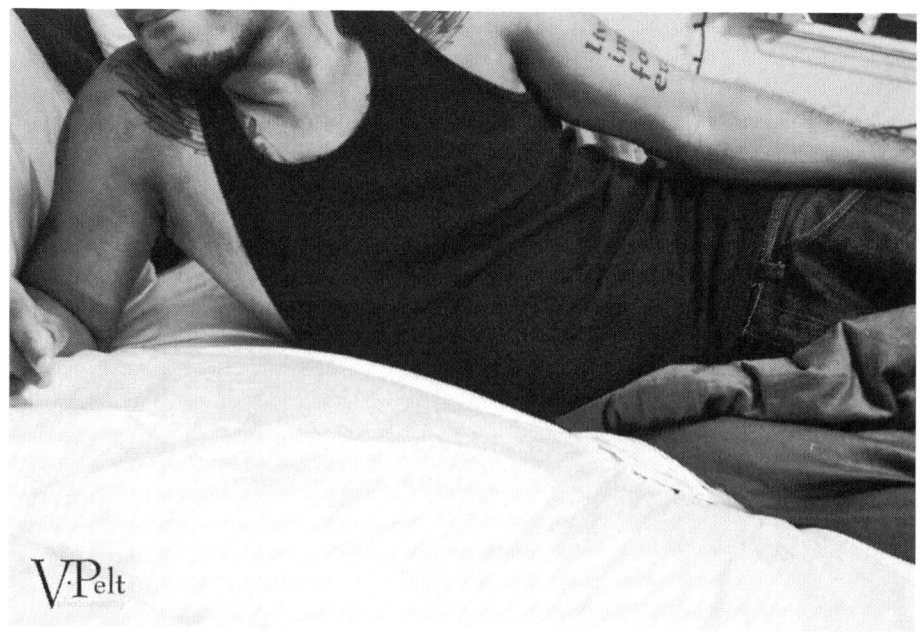

V·P_{elt}

A wink, a tease, a tickle..

Each seem to have magical powers. I am a woman, passionate, feeling like a sorceress, in a very public space. From this bar stool, I appear to rest, but stir with reckless thoughts. I can see you. In tailored clothes, you stand with a short glass filled with your liquor and a few cubes. This room is dim, but I can imagine you are still quite mysterious with the lights on. Your shadow reveals the outline of your well-defined frame.

I notice many of your distinctions, particularly the curves and points in your face, which I feign to touch. Like abstract art, I'd make my own sense of you, and make sense of however I want it or you... You scan the room and catch me staring, you look away initially, but curiosity slowly draws you back to a pair of intrigued eyes. You fight it, looking over your shoulder. Then, you look back once more and you've been snagged. You relax. Bewitched, you appear to be enchanted. I move toward you snaking my way through the dim, crowded room, eyes still on you, I put my hand on top of yours and I move my lips across your face. I get close, but there is no touch. Suddenly, my cheek rests on yours as my lips creep towards your ear. You smell my perfume and feel my breath against your sensitive skin. I tickle your ear with a whisper. Magically you are mine. You follow my curves through the crowd and when we pause you hesitate, but little by little become comfortable with the feel of your hand holding my hip.

One...

in the AM. Bare skin pressed to bare skin, our legs tangled, and our arms locked, we fell asleep...In the early hours of the morning I turn over and see you sleeping in the dark. The shadows dancing across your lips intensify my desire. I creep closer. I watch your chest rise and fall, imagining your heart the passionate center of my sexiest fantasies and desires.

Come inside....

And you'll find us, as we lie next to the words and let them tickle our thoughts with fantasies and daydreams. They've been used and thus taken out with me many times. I return them later with the scent of passion's perfumes to write some more under covers smeared with ink and scraps of paper. A novella of poetry stimulated by a stream of intense fantasy both actualized and neglected. Together, intimately bound in the pages of the same book, they entangle themselves into one passionate story.

Now curious reader, follow along this poetic journey, a love story of a different kind, one of raw desire and furious romance. As you continue down a steamy street you notice it is aroused with sultry lovers engulfed in a haze of sensation: smudging up the streets, pressing and smearing against brick walls and chain-link fences. You look to the left and see us leaning up against a sports car, a couple of hot, impassioned lovers. We are sweaty, pulling at each other's hair and clothes, lip-locked. Further down the asphalt you'll find it's worn with mystery, scars, intimacy, and amorous and hedonic encounters. You make eye contact with us. Our body language suggests that you loosen up. You welcome it. We strip. And so do you, leaving all your insecurities near that remote light post and chase along with us, reckless with our love, desires, and acts, chronicled through the poems plastered across the pages to follow.....

RECKLESS INCLINATIONS

I CARESSES

II DEVIATION

III INTOXICATED

IV CARNAL

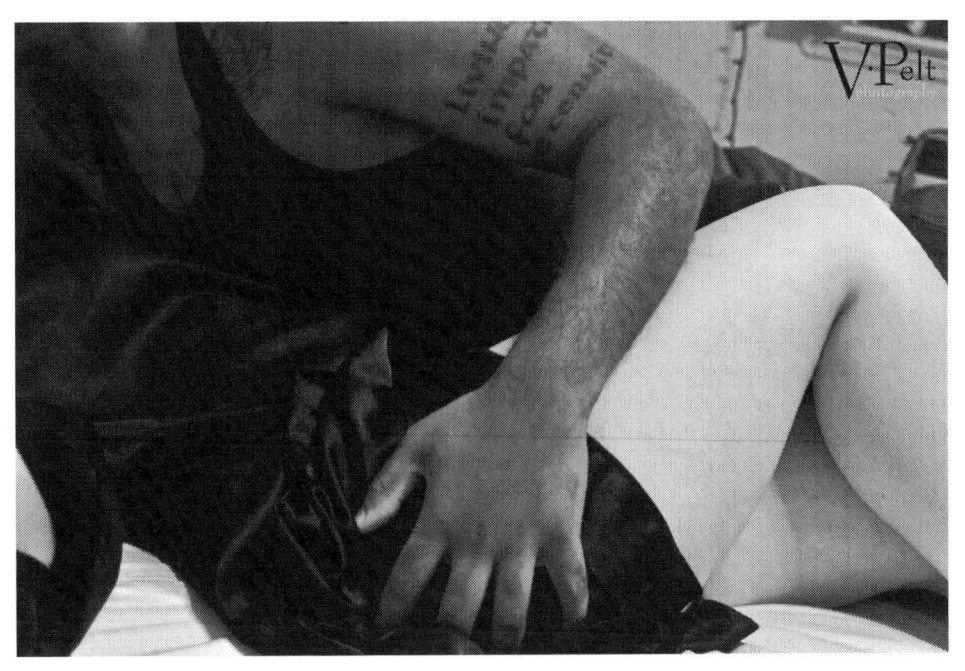

I
CARESSES

Some touches go deep, making eternal indentations on the heart. Even with your eyes, we touch. Your stare blows a tingly sensation down my arms when you look at me in awe and tell me that across your bare chest is where I belong. I take you inside my robe. We embrace in a sequence of slow, affectionate motions. In bed I straddle your silky, lower back, where it dips like a saddle. I'm a perfect fit and together we compose a melody of sensations. It's an organic connection of which we caress, blend, and concoct a rhythm. I begin to massage your aches and tensions. Pressing deep with passionate fingers and palms, I make waves in your subconscious where we exist as romantic creatures. We are timeless.. weightless.. fearless. Bred from a luscious stock of lovers. We tumble, roll and switch positions.

CARESSES

Your whispered words are cool
little breaths of purifying air
that caress my heart,
smoothening out the rough roads
twisted and wrapped around the bottom
of the treacherous mountains in my soul

Your eyes caress my deepest,
darkest, and most endless spaces.
Unafraid, you rub and massage,
mending them closed
in a dark room lit by only
a single candle

Your kisses caress the butterflies
In my chest and stomach.
You tickle them as you dance with them,
singing a love song
Slowly rocking your hips
back and forth

All your celestial caresses

make my hips do a wave

opening my eyes wide enough

to see the infinite dark sky.

I play in the constellations,

feeling like I am one with the stars.

SECRET PUDDLES

Secrets tickle my skin.

I giggle them into the clouds

and let them soak me

when they fall with

the rain,

dripping slowly

from my dark curly waves,

                pouring into

            dark puddles

        reflecting the moon

             and stars.

             I stir them

                and

           watch them

              reappear.

           My memory

         draws our stars

           in the dark

            reflection.

        Deep in the sky

              I watch

             your lips

on replay

whispering in the rain.

Over my glossy skin,

drip,

drop,

drip.

Tickling the ground

dampening and loosening solidified lust

HIGHJACK

You opened up the white sheets

of your most intimate slumber and let me

crawl

underneath

where I could squeeze myself in and slide deep to the

bottom of your wildest desires,

highjack your restrained dreams,

press all the buttons in your cockpit,

take the captain hostage,

fly upside down, backwards,

and spin out of control.

Full-speed… we fly straight to our destination

arriving at Earth's highest peak

and descend slowly in a parachute.

BENCH LOVE

My eyes blended into yours

On a bench

worn with history

smudged with love

smeared with some intimacy

pressed and rolled over with kisses

lusty eyes have photographed it countless times

In the square under the sun it tans

content in its place it watches

the sun rise and fall

The light of the moon cools its steamy heat

sparkly cobblestones reflect blue

attracting couples

lip and finger-locked to take a seat

this bench sees no deformities,

no ends,

and no mysteries,

but only cultivates the gardens

in the hearts of lusty,

loving Spain

NATURALLY PLAYFUL

When I hold you down
I am a lioness grown,
with a jungle of experience
a strong woman pinning her man
to a dreamy cloud of mattress
adored and pleasured by her pride,
for she fills them up with Juicy, red
carnage.

Looking down at your bare chest
I imagine a lightning storm
of electric explosions
grip your wrists tight
let myself go a little wild.
I play,
nipping you
then licking your wounds,
kissing you up
until I can give your face a real, deep stare
suddenly, I am taken away to foreign lands
perceiving you and I as an adventure,

a safari of exotic plants and animals.

In those green eyes
I see myself,
a little girl
rolling in tall green grass
in the rolling plains
with the sun on my face
giggling like I do with you in bed.

QUEEN

You treat me like an Egyptian queen.
My naked body covered in gold plates and colored
jewels.
I lay on my belly swinging my bare legs,
while you feed me laden, succulent
purple grapes.
On your pearly bed where I pose so confidently as if
it's my marble thrown.
I look satisfyingly victorious and close my eyes
as you kiss my hand.
I dream of nothing,
but immortality.
In your eyes
I am a rare, exotic cat
in an Egyptian royal family
kept for religious worship.

LOVER OF TIME

Lover-

The watch I wear has stopped.

My moon-eyes gaze above the roof top.

The brightness blinds me during the day.

These hands, frozen for eternity pray.

I find comfort only in this empty black sea,

where I swim, look down, and loose myself.

Lover-

I put the dead watch

in a bottle and gave it to a wave.

Inside I feel as if I took that bottle

chewed and swallowed-

your memory

I'll forever save

as a painful digestion

think it life's tainted selection.

Lover-

I saw you open my bottled time in my dreams

My cries have been muted

so you can't hear me scream.

You put on my dead watch,

admiring it and such

It began to tick with your touch….

In the distance I hid in the sand dunes

watching in awe

knowing I'd awaken soon.

BUTTERFLY DREAMING

I wrap myself in linens made of Persian thread.

I am cocooned:

A plain caterpillar

yearning to transform into an exotic butterfly,

wakeup another woman…

a much more sensual one.

Having flown all over

a dreamland of creamy clouds

this particular morning I awaken feeling sexier,

disappointed that I have little recollection of what I've

dreamt about.

CANDY CANES

Reds & greens
kiss as they
twist
to the last jolly lick-
slipping through

the fingers

of the woman with the peppermint
flavored lips,
white lights
flickering behind her
cherry colored dress,
she stares into the chocolate
with the grassy tin wrapping

until it begins to resemble
mistletoe as she makes
two candy canes kiss

and form a heart<3

LUST FLAKES

Lust

                                              Flakes

                                                                               Fall

                                                                             At Contact

Vulnerable

                                        Frosty lips

                                                                               Warm

Frost Bitten

                                            Eyes

THE HOLE IN MY SWEATER

I stare through the hole you burnt in my sweater.

The result of your love for a loosey

with your liquor.

Now a peephole,

It's a time warp-

I rub my finger on its singed center

retrieving moments of a night a few years ago

A lick-

chased with a lime.

Free spirits dance in the colored lights.

I watch you,

with your crazy, sexy, cool..

that made me breathless in the dark.

Chain linked fingers dangle about the crowd.

Your eyes as deep as mine,

we were bent,

twisting and diving into each other's pupils.

We were strangers

taking our four-block walk home.

From the dance floor
to the grass, we were
catching, netting and jarring up
fast swimming rebound kisses.

I have forty other sweaters,
but refuse to part from this one
or sew it up.

Worn, abused, burnt
it hangs in my closet for safekeeping
like an old photo,
a note in a box full of memories.
I wear it occasionally
when I do, I roll up the hole
into a cuff in my sleeve.
If they saw, it I could no longer mean
the same to me.
Alone I unroll it,
gazing through my little peep hole-
Dreaming. Remembering. Rearranging.

HOLIDAY SKY

Hanging from the moon,
Wrapped in lace.
Above the trees
sprinkled with white lights.
Icy stars mapping out the sky,
you watch the pink sunsets
glowing in my dark eyes

GEMS AND STONES

Alone,

I swallowed emotional stones

and felt them tumble

down my throat and through my chest

causing tears to swim to my surface

and my eyes to get glossy

when the thought about

how you make me feel

cherished when you held me

in your hands like a precious gemstone.

I tickle your ears with promises

whispering

How I want to be

your yellow, tourmaline sun

shining on your skin with warmth.

How I want to be

your red, ruby heart

beating excitedly.

Or how my lips will forever

roll smoothly over yours

like light pink pearls
when we kiss.

Oh, how I want to be
your blue, sapphire sky
so you can draw constellations
on me with your fingers.
I want to keep
your green, peridot eyes
alive
when I water your driest crevices.

Alone,
my eyes are watering
because in your face I see truth.
I see your appreciation.
I see potential.
So, love,
keep me close to your heart
and you'll forever have value.

FOREIGN ROOTS

I asked you to fill me up
with your organic coconut water.
Softly kiss my rosy face,
Passionately bite my orchid lips,
And slowly
Pour yourself
into my deepest holes
I whisper these words as I lie
in a tangled garden
of overgrown fantasies
without an almanac.
There are strange plants growing
from the soils of my subconscious.
Foreign: they've no roots in the earth,
leaning towards sparkling stars

pointing their teal petals,
directing my eyes
towards another universe.

GYPSY LOVE

In this small town of no ones
my eyes grab onto many familiar souls,
while I skip like a gypsy drunk off love potion
with my long curly locks
twisting behind me in the wind.
                    Wild,
         I run free in my animal print tee,
   stop young men in their cars and they freeze
            ..even in this summer heat
       my gaze locks them in like a lioness
           who spots a piece of meat
             Still with a heart beat...
             Boom...Boom...Boom.

There's a drum in my head.
It's got a rhythm.
My gypsy soul has taken over.
Hold your necklaces and watches.
I will strip you of your valuables
just to hold you close...*stranger*...
Then I disappear into the crowd.
I am too an unknown in this small town.

WARM AND COLD BLOODED

I'm the vampire in your werewolf dreams...
You tickle my goose bumps
when I whine for blood.
I never shiver because my skin is always cold.

I pet you,

as you rest up against me.

I say:

Oh please boy..

stay

be my fur coat

and I'll swallow any silver bullets in your path.

Sacrifice a little for me-
Hunt to satisfy my hunger.
Tonight, lick the wounds in my heart clean
and I'll love you forever.

MAKING HISTORY

Looking around the room
I took notice of the artifacts
that define our era
and think of us as a part of the antiquity of now.
We are creating an atom of eternity,
a sexy 21st century
love affair,
with all the markings of its time.

When you touch my naked face to your lips
I wonder if I could've been more passionate in past
lifetimes,
had I lived without
all our conveniences and luxuries.
This could be all we know or an illusion,
this free-loving feeling that twists
my thoughts
all the while bound and tied down
by exotic and diverse things in this city
like lace ties and handcuffs.

You're mine with the press of a button,
a click, or a text.
It's modern sorcery.
We are equally objectified,
Changing clothes,
wearing costumes for each other
quickly becoming just another device
replaceable,
like my digital camera and cell phone.
I look into your body language searching for the
possibility of camouflaged romance,
trying my hardest to see traces of it
like an optical illusion
in the lines of your flexed arms.

II
DEVIATION

I lie in my comforters and imagine my body undergoing an evolution. I am tickled, poked and kinky thoughts are born. They grow and come to life. With closed eyes, I unfold... and discover that I am a capricious creature in a peculiar world. Flashbacks of your eyes... your skin.. your scars. Images of our exclusive moments are posted on the walls of this fantasy world. Rapture runs down my face, hangs on my lips and lingers in frustration picturing how your tongue played with my fingers. My lips are pressed against my arms... fantasizing.. it is you and I. I am kissing your poetic tattoos... those deep words engraved on your otherwise pure skin. Your presence is erected somewhere between legs and sheets. It's supernatural. You appear in front of me and before your eyes I shed my skin and transform....

BORN OF ROSES & SCORPIONS

Your Scorpio seductive potions nurtured
my Libra baby bird feathers
showing me the fantasies and magic powers
of being a woman.

My mother painted her lips red
with a crimson colored lipstick
attracting the darkest scorpions
spawned deep
in the souls of men young and old.

Off her red lips songbirds pranced
after flying from the vines of her vocals.
In those songs, a baby bird,
saw the curves of the woman
I'd one day see in the mirror.
It was my mother...
only with a few exotic roots.
She is a woman with darker features.

The birds sung my heart to sleep many nights and

carried me to places

where I was a sacred princess

treasured by a kingdom of knights and maidens. Her

songs planted seeds that would only grow,

flowering into wild passion flowers.

In bed I lay,

a rare bird,

naked with a sexy warrior.

Gazing into his rough skin

thinking of where I came from...

I picture a beautiful red rose

in a romance with an onyx scorpion.

HATCHED

A light grew in my chest and slowly
ate away at my cold exterior.
My vampire skin cracked for weeks,
secreting strange liquids
from my broken crevices ..

I dripped them all around town,
all on my friends,
all naked with you in bed
and turned you off.

Shattered open,
I'm here-
hatched,
making new promises to myself.

My feelings walk bare-naked in public,
dancing alone in a crowd
to a sexy techno song.
Proud.

I hang up my innocent,
good girl hats-
the ones with the polka dots and hearts
and trade them in for outlandish,
badass, purple hair extensions.

Today I'm flying with all my strength,
intelligence,
self-healing powers,
and free loving nature,
like a precious bird
with diamond encrusted wings
and golden feathers.

ZOMBIE-GIRL

Have another!
Cheers!
Raise your glass and swallow happiness!
Lay a thick layer of film over that emptiness!
Be like us!

Tired of listening
Deaf ears writing prescriptions
I squirm out of the arms of conformity
like a stubborn child.

> *Zombie thoughts....*
> *Zombie talk...*
> *Zombie dreams..*

Bungee jumping off the earth's ledge
-A sampling of free.
Tired of running
they'll catch me,
my eyes will freeze and be lost forever-
Another victim to their slavery.

CAMOUFLAGED

I see jungles in your eyes,

while tasting the condensation

on your lips

as I suck the steam

from your mouth

communicating in animalistic tongues.

You play and hide from me,

but not for long.

I follow your scent:

    Burberry..

And we sit by a hot pool

trading signs,

body language,

as we smudge each other with war paint.

When you look at me

I feel like I'm wearing army fatigues.

You can't see me.

My insecurities are taken as prisoners of war

and I am camouflaged.

LOST FOR LOVE

We broke up against walls that refused to fall.

There are fragments of brick on my black jacket.

I carry the pieces

reminding me of the indentations

you've left on me,

the white residue that splattered

when you were rough,

called me names,

made me feel ashamed,

then said I was to blame.

Still broken, bruised, and beaten with verbiage,

I wear dark sunglasses to feel free.

I am without words.

There's nothing I can say….

In your arms I was somebody else,

a lost girl,

a hopeless romantic

taken hostage while on a search for her love story.

REINVENTION

I want to reinvent myself,
color my hair
then cut it all off,
get a blond wig with black streaks,
and live the life of a freak
a few days a week.

Imma remix myself
be more lusciously,
sexual,
emotionally tolerable,
look even hotter in a t-shirt,
find a man who is dangerously irresistible,
and be more aggressive
and vulgar with the fellas

I'm rewiring my connections,
masquerading around
with 6 different masks
in my back pocket,
experimenting with voodoo,

and admitting that I'm hot for dreadlocks.

I am NEW…

Making a vow to be fearless,

more attentive,

more intuitive,

I will breathe each breath

like it's sacred H20,

look deeper into the eyes of others,

cleanse,

wash away the anxiety,

regrets, & phobias,

get a psychic reading

ask for an exorcism,

bow to the gods

and start anew.

PLAYED

He says I played him.
I told him I don't play games,
I'm not a child, but a woman.

I'll burn stacks of cards
before your eyes
and shout
"deuces!!!"

I traded in my chess
for a Ouija board
Now, I experiment with my body's
supernatural powers.

My words are a bit bewitching,
as I can't stop the vulgar language
falling from my lips.
Yes, he brings out my primitive nature.
I rough him up,
                 knock him out,
and ruffle his feathers.

PIECES

I couldn't fix our love.

I didn't understand the mechanics.

I was confused by its parts.

Screwed...

The screwdriver couldn't fix this one.

You can't fix something you never understood.

Tell me everything you know about these pieces.

<u>Tell me</u>

Did it break in ha/lf,

f/o/u/rs,

or s h a t t e r?

These pieces in my palms are misfits,

sharp and jagged.

My hands are bloody.

I wash them down with some of your tears.

I'm drained.

My pulse is slowing.

I need to bandage up and get the hell out-

I'm gone!

RED TEARS

In the shadows
a red rose bleeds
weeping as it wilts away.

Suffocating vines
take
their last breaths.

White walls stifle
colorful dreams.
I dip my hands in these red tears
and like brushing a canvas
I paint your eyes on my blank wall.

THE RULES RULE

The Rules:
Break them and fall,
Hard not to be so sinful,
Dare not be loud and needy,
only sneak behind the scenery
Spinning. Agonizing. Wishing
Fighting with the limitations
--thoughts imprisoned--
Sex-fiend is wearing her stripes
sitting on a bench
Chatting with Miss. Commitment
about how thunder and lightning turn them on,
spitting on the prison guards that make
love so damn hard!
Broke the rules-
Cage me, like the animal I am
and make me serve my time

BURNING PLASTIC

Phony.

Plastic.

Labeled the "perfect" American WOMAN

This Barbie stole G.I. Joe's Jeep

Packed it with her plastic pumps,

bows, and babies

Drove it down the hall

far from the pink house and pink corvette

straight towards the kitchen

with a scissor she cuts her long blond

locks and throws them in the trunk,

dumps hairspray out over it all

to the beat of a heavy metal song

a lit match is tossed from the counter top

as she leans against a bottle of Jack,

smokes with Cat Woman

holding the flames of the melting jeep

in her eyes

POST BREAKUP

It's over....

        Light a match,

        lie back,

        and WATCH all our bullshit

        burn up in clouds of dark smoke-

        When the dust settles,

        I'll be covered in soot.

        Dancing in this tragedy,

        painting white walls

        with my fingers,

        touching myself,

        as I eye every warm, male body

                outside of this room.

Looking to pull them in,

        I imagine that

        I will twist with them,

        tangle with them ,

        and go way too far,

like we never could....

        Now I do everything, but regret

        not asking to be tied to the bedpost.

REFLECTIONS ON A BROKEN COFFEE CUP

In the morning pink lips make love
to broken coffee cups,
with memories of your stiff cuffs and buttons
at war with
my unpaired necklaces and earrings,
as I sit in Indian style on the bed.

You only buy American cars,
support the war,
and may have dumped me
because of your love affair with G.W.

I am not your kind of refined.
This is fine,
I think, as I stain my teeth
with this coffee that tastes so much
better than your lips.

You still try to call me crazy
when you call on the phone
and I speak my mind,
which drives you even crazier.
Then, you hang up.

I celebrate,
throwing about
notepaper like confetti
with my scribbles of
hate, love, and nonsense
written all over them.
I release them irrationally
in the middle of the room
in spite of you and
your scent that I can
still smell on my pillow.

FACEBOOK HAUNTING

I'm still haunted by the connection

we felt when we danced all those nights

under strobe lights,

took shots of Jose Cuervo,

and wandered home

stumbling under street lights.

Your eyes are so deep.

I remember all the dreams I've had of them

and those wet, beautiful lips….

I can't get the music out of my head

that played in the background!

Your sexy pics… I melt….

Then, I delete you from my friends list.

Now you're but a ghost that pops-up in

my newsfeed.

It haunts me at the emptiest of times

when I need the electricity to charge me

like the sparks that fired from our friction.

…..Damn social networking…..

IN THE CLUB

I hate your antics almost as much
as your self-absorbed, self-loving tendencies.
I can't control the destructive impulses
I get when I see you make love
to yourself in front of the digital camera.
The impulses I used to have
that once were very sexual.
I despise
the way the strobe lights
dance in your dark glasses.
You know you're so hot-
You allow not a single hair to have a flaw.
The music plays
you shove me away,
cross the dance floor,
grab a sexy Latina,
swing her around,
pull her lips close to yours,
and make me crazy.
I let some exotic man
take my hand and grind on me.

Later on I'll text your drunk ass.
And tell you how this shit is gonna be
BTW U N ME
you call my words *reckless*....
I know I am...
Also a little crazy...
I wear my little tube dress
like a straitjacket
shakin my ass in VIP
with strangers-
my new Italian Sistas,
who sweat the way I wreck
this dance floor,
and show me much love <3
They say I should leave you here,
but I take you home.
You still call me
a hoe
And I say... SO?

III

INTOXICATED

Glass in hand, I shout "here's to all the ladies called reckless for showing too much emotion!" I throw it back and see a flash of your face, a close up, as clear as any photo. I am a sorceress when intoxicated. I can do magic and you are here. In your eyes I saw an expedition, one that would distort my thoughts. Many times we met on the same floor, drunken, sloppy, but sexy, lit under a strobe light.

> Shaking {fast} rocking...rocking...rocking...I squeeze your shoulder and run my hand slowly down to your belt loop and hold on, gripping, and then slam up against your solid flesh and take your short whispered sentences like shots

When you show up you find me dancing alone, running my hands from my hips to my head and back down. You take me by the hand and think me a lush. You've said it before...I am a wreck with these words I spill all over you. But all these words are the truth.

COCKTAIL

Limes and clear, silver tequila

look at the sterling sparkles in my eyes.

It's clear

that you drive me to drink

Concoct me a cock-tail

to grapple with these fantastic thoughts.

I can't get your body's curves

out of my head.

I named this drink

ENTANGLEMENT

Ingredients:

1 shot me,

1 shot of you,

rocks,

a dash of lime juice

Directions:

stir, shake, and pour slow

Touch me.

Pre-game on top of me.

Get me drunk

and then drink me down,

make my heart numb

and give me a wicked hangover.

VENOMOUS POSSESSION

Sunk your sharp teeth in
and told me how good they felt inside.
I thought he should take them out
but the pain was satisfying .
My lower back twitched,
as if I was possessed,
striking the hard floor
then jolting up and coming to an abrupt stop
before striking again.
You found me dressed in a buttoned-up cartigan.
The scent of your venom secretes from my pores
I smell it, pressing my nose to my forearms.
You brought me back to life
in the death of a sexually rejected,
insecure girlfriend.
I look in the mirror
in this sexy hotel room and I see
red, erotic scenes in my eyes,
my hair untamed,
lips so seductive,
as I pucker at myself in the mirror.

CAN'T STOP

Can't stop...

Listening to the R&B,

writing poetry,

breathing in hot steam,

dancing through the night until the sun is seen,

drinking until I forget it all,

spinning until I fall.

Can't stop...

I'm anxious,

extremely hazardous,

speeding on the highway in a RUSH,

my body is numb; I'm a lush.

Can't stop...

I'm a reckless lover,

forgetful as all hell,

unprofessional in all worlds,

passionate, but strangely senseless.

Can't stop...

Self-medicating a rejected body,

stripping my armor,

RUNNING raw...

ADDICTED

Craving reckless passion,
I poison my veins with adrenaline
and smoke your breath
until my lungs get cloudy.

**Your eyes are drawn in permanent marker
onto the walls of my subconscious.**

Obsessively I write your name *ROUGH*

                              with a pink Sharpee

I rip out the pages,
in my sketch book
fold them up,
and put them in my hearts deepest pockets.

My skin quivers when I swim for days on end
in the dark seas of my pillows and sheets
that we slept in together.

Tell me you want me again.

Grab my hand,

tickle my tongue,

squeeze my lips with yours,

hold my fingers close,

Call me:

sexy

FICTION

My first glimpse
caught stars
and blinded my rigid walk.
I stumbled sober,
but quickly caught myself
watching the streetlights
glow in your eyes
and reflect in broken glass
on the cement.

                              My red slinky shirt
                              dripped off the edge
                              of my shoulders
                              and hung on loosely.
                              Scooping up the straps
                              of my shirt
                              I lost sight of you.

Busy night feet,
Busy artists,
working on smoke smudged,
gum vandalized pavement
through the night,

pushing through
the collages of New York's
dirty breath.

Time moves slower than usual
as we cross paths over and over.
We talk again
over shot glasses of poison
that glow in the darkness,
empower us to reminisce
and create fiction.

                        You were a mind reader,
                    a sorcerer with magical powers
               smoothly catching the thoughts
                 that spilled from my eyes and
                         pour them back into
                          my half empty glass.
                           Luring me in deep
                          you then paralyze me

and send me
off into the dark
and thick streets
completely disoriented.

LUST THIRSTY

Got bit by that mosquito

on the porch

that summer night.

I didn't resist the little vampire;

Let it pierce my skin.

So good

A lonely anesthetic lives within me.

I hate needles,

but

love the anticipation

of pain.

Satisfied

with its easy thievery,

flying into the depths of the sky

lost among its doubles,

equal

and identical

in every way.

KISSING FLAKES

His cold

Avalanche words

Freeze

My

Winter lips

Now

I

Kiss

Flakes

Under the influence

Of hypothermia

SILENT CONFESSIONS

What could you do- If I confessed,

cleaned up our mess,

and stopped pretending

never gave back that t-shirt you lent me?

And if proved you right,

threw a fit tonight,

pushed you off me,

laid out the truth nicely,

and denied your eyes?

I've decided to walk away

What should you do- If I throw away phoniness,

accepted loneliness,

laughed at your lies,

let myself cry,

enjoyed a taste of fate,

and even felt sorry for you?

From now on I'll look away

What would you do- If I got over you,

moved on too,

forgot that song,

admitted to myself that you were wrong,

erased you from my dreams,

thought of something else before I fell asleep,

and broke all the promises I said I'd keep?

Tonight I have driven miles to lock you away

ABUSIVE

Dear Poetry,

I've abused you, dragged you in and chained you
to my darkest hours. I soaked you all up to get drunk
off you.....
Shot you back with salt and lime to wash you down my
esophagus...
down
to
my
stomach
so you could share the anxiety, excitement, frustration,
wonder, and pain.

When my mind is sick I let you spill from my lips like
vomit......involuntarily.

PASSION IS MY POISON

Passion is my poison.

I write words at the rate my heart pumps blood.

Mine have no rhythm or pulse, but they have soul.

They have a spirit with no plan in mind.

Passion is my poison.

It turns my insides all different colors.

They are a mood ring or a healing stone.

I once thought I was a witch.

Now, I am convinced I am just passionate.

Passion is my poison.

Oceans move me.

Leaves on the trees make decisions for me.

A beautiful pair of eyes can captivate me.

And I often seem stoned when I'm sober

Passion is my poison.

I crave feelings as most crave chocolate or cheese.

There is no luck.. only fate.

My soul feels and sees things from other worlds.

Passion is my poison.

I can't sleep at night.

Some of my thoughts take time to come to a boil.

I stare at the ceiling plotting how I'll get the next toxin.

IV

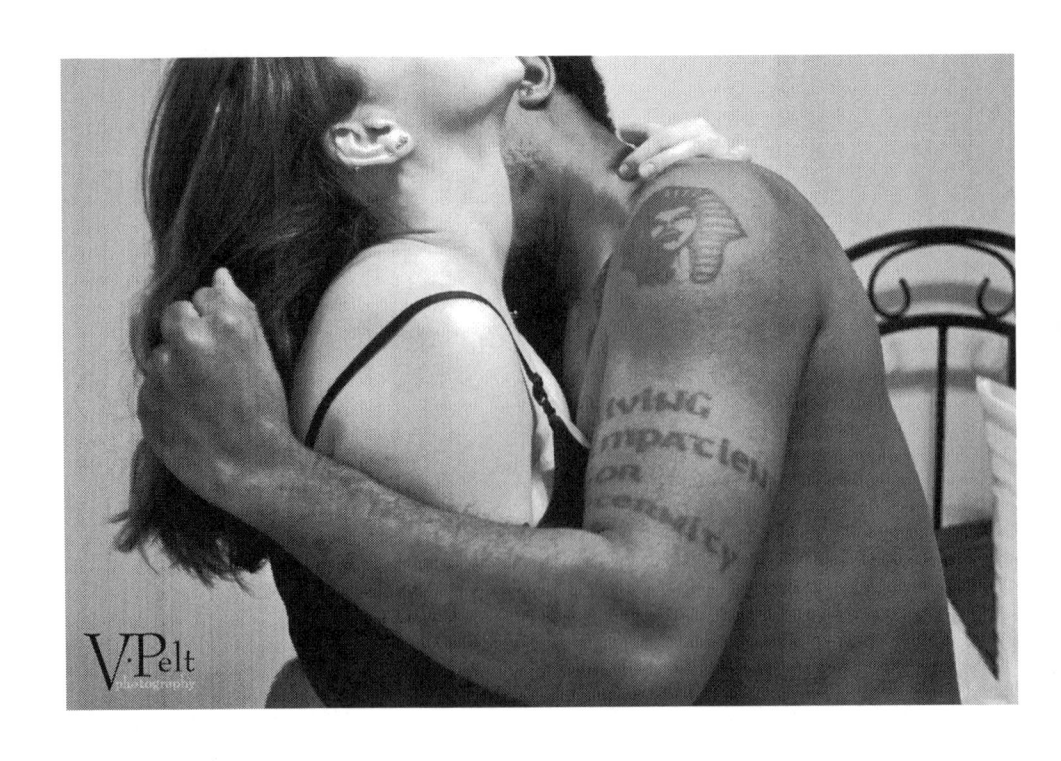

CARNAL

Pouring... flooding.. rushing water runs over my shoes like a river and eventually slips between my toes. Through the rain I see you walking towards me in the distance. Drops of rain fall to my skin. I shine... glossy in my habitat. I am an indigenous woman, with bobcat like qualities. Feeling quite savage, I hone in on you, alone, caught in this sultry shower. We sizzle... soaked... rain slipping and sliding down our sleek arms. I suck the raindrops from your lips- you taste sweet and salty. Unable to hold your wet skin tight enough, I grab your sopping white wife beater, grip, and pull you closer. Its a raw scene. Were in the wild...My fingernails press against the back of your neck and scratch through your hair gently while you move your hands down and pull/ hold onto on my lace thong. It's a raw scene. We're two dark creatures in this monsoon. In the wild...There

are no thoughts, just bodies reacting to nature..
I pull you towards shelter we peel each
others' saturated clothes off. Your smell is
comfort, an aphrodisiac, a drug all in one. I
imagine climbing you like a tree and holding tight
pressing my chest against your sticky sap.

INSTINCT

Snakeskin, red lights, foam, and champagne bubbles
Flicker, flicker
goes our sun-kissed skin
in mirrored ceilings and walls.
Wet lips dance together over hot steam.

                                      You grab me
                                  and I watch me,
                                        watch you,
                                          watch us,
                                  in the reflections,
                                  like a hot porno.

It's so instinctual,
Rough and sensual
we touch wildly bathing in a hot pool.
I envision a romance in
the thick of a green scene
and we're the only man and woman
for miles in a jungle full of snakes and jaguars.

No clothes.

We're primal.

Thirsty: kiss me

Hungry: nibble me

If it gets too cold and wet,

rub two sticks together

and were on fire…

RELEASE ME

Reckless, I am falling wildly into you.
Restless, I can't stop thinking of your lips.
Regretting, each time I'm vulnerable too.
Releasing, stress and tension into your arms.
My Heart, is beating so heavily- complications.
In the air like freeing a dove,
your words gave me peace
if *only for a night or two.*

                                         Take me bottled up
                                            like aging wine
                                            and pour me slow....

We can just twist, wind, and shake
on the way *down*
to the floor.

                                                    I'm on Fire!
                                  There are fireballs in my chest.
                                      Bouncing off my heart
                              they spin around in my rib cage
                    lighting the fires of the sleeping beauties
                                                  in my soul.

I hear the dragons screaming

as they blow their flames:

Skeeeeooouuuk!!!!!

Skreeeeeen!!!!!!

Skiiia!!!!!!!!

My heart gurgles:

Bulooop!

Buloop!

Bulop!

Crushed:

Says my soul, with a strangled whisper.

The sound of the words are poison
and I take them like shots of tequila
at a Tiki bar in a hurricane.

Love-wooooooo

The wind is whispering in my ear.

woooooooo-Love

Spinning in the rain
I whisper: *put it out.*

HIT ME UP

Hit me

up.

...dial tone...

Ring!

Ring!

buzz:::buzz:::

You touch me with a text.

The sexy little digital letters

tickle my cheeks.

I smile so big

it hurts.

You're too good

it's bad for my health.

It's a colorful pill,

an anticipated thrill

Hunger:

I need you in me.

You're my OCD.

It's an over-dose.

I'm an addict.

Sell me some secretly.

this can't be legal

give me more:

under the table,

in my closet,

in your car,

in your dark room,

on a wooded path,

or here alone in these sheets…

press the keys # 516 *

Hit me up

I just want to hear the voice of my man.

Call me

and don't ever hang up the phone.

SEXT

U call me a FREAK

{pause}

Then tell me what u'll do 2 me

slowly on Monday

sending each juicy detail

throughout the day

the ringing messages

make my lips tingle

rough words on Tuesday

I can imagine the floor shaking

softly on Wednesday

I feel a ticklish sensation

running from my chest to my toes

at my desk

thursday I think this is not like me....

this texting is naughty

but who needs to know

where these conversations go

I can feel the words

hear them as little whispers

from your mind

I admit it……

I just recently started

to F*ckin love it

shhhh… don't tell NE1

when U text me:

where r my pics

what u waitn 4 grl?

I text u back *LMFAO*

wishin I had the gutz

to send you somethin

X-RATED

like you just did…

I reply: winking smiley-face

U drive me CRAZY

in the physical

we are free, loose,

f*ckin unattached

afterwards we text

in real life

our words touch

analyze and conceptualize

then, it all gets complicated,

connected, and emotional

sext me

I become UR freaky

dream girl

in a rain storm of sexts

and all the complications

screw each other into oblivion

NEEDY

If you ask my friends,

they will tell you sweetie

I'm not needy,

but I do need you next to me

before I fall sleep,

I need to lie across your chest,

feel your heart beat.

Let it make me rush, rush,

Suck, suck, an adrenaline lollipop.

You make me sticky.

Taste the cherry flavor on my lips.

Get pieces of candy stuck in my curly hair.

I need to close my eyes

like a little girl and imagine

what it would be like

to wake up next to you

in the morning.

I need to be

needed by a sexy man,

a man that needs to be

needed by a sexy me.

He needs to want me,

to stand with a strong lady against the world

and melt like a teenager when he touches

me alone behind closed doors.

My eyes blink into yours as yours

sparkle into mine,

showing reflections of the others

as we press, kneed, and grind.

It's only sex- *yes* –but you ask

what's next for our electric connection,

then you black out if I show too much interest.

Stop picking apart our wires

come get locked in

and I'll give you the spare keys.

I am a dreamer,

a believer.

I am not needy.

Come with me

to sleep.

4 AM

Exhaling the damp night air,
breath staggering in its thickness,
eyes deep and wide swallow the ceiling
dreaming of the perfect kitchen-knife
and how precisely I could remove
the sharp pains in my chest
that are embedded like jagged metal splinters.

I'd cut around their edges,
carve them out before they cover over and scab.
I'll crack them open and watch
drips of red drops
pour, dribble and drop down my skin
wet...

I could finger-paint and draw red pictures,
but that would be sick....*wouldn't it?*
And you would commit me,
make it official and certify me
if you heard just a sentence
of my consciousness.

Your mind is so perfectly sound
you'd know exactly what to do.
You are rational
or maybe you'd surprise me,
take matters into your own hands
and tie my hands up,
prevent me from hurting myself.

I would tell you it was *sexy* to piss you off
because you'd know it was the truth
                        I whisper: *Verdaderamente sexy*
                                  Veramante sexy
And then you may cover my mouth
to shut me up....even sexier.

If I exposed my night life
to your day's flawless white light,
you would try to civilize me,
force me to behave rationally,
and admit that
there are no foreign objects
beneath my cracking skin.
Then what is it that makes me creep

between the sheets while you sleep?

Denial?

You must know I deceive you.

I am no porcelain-doll.

Cant you see?

My hair is wild.

I have

scraped-up knees,

and knuckles.

I'm broken.

An insomniac.

A heat-rock.

You rest peacefully deep,

while jealousy begs my choked dreams

to laugh deviously at me

and you'll never know

I toss and turn,

shake myself-up,

make my insides

rain and dampen

the dried blood

in my soul.

Only during the day are there times

I think you may know.

When the sun hits my face

you see the little red scars

marked into my eye's dark browns.

My pupils are screaming at a frequency

that you cannot pickup.

Tonight –burning,

eyes tearing,

I whisper:

"put me out"

into your sleeping ears.

My heart races and I hold my wrist

to check for a pulse: *Beat. Beat. Beat.*

Alive….

The bloody currents inside me rush violently

I grip onto you.

Cryptic-touch-demonic-lust-

I mumble
strange words
as I singe
the end
of your tee-shirt,
with the fire
in my fingertips,
frustrated since you last touched my lips.

Lying next to you,
lying to myself-
to bring down the flames,
blowing heat into the small strips of light
that pierce the blinds
striking my eyes,
like matches.
I pull the covers over my head,
crawl back to you,
pressing my cheek to your chest
bringing down the temperature
of my burning interior.

CRAZY

My rosy, blushed cheeks
pressing up against my fiery, brown eyes.
My friends no longer recognize me.
I smear my eye shadow
under my eyes
like war paint
and tell them
"Yes, it's all different now."
I'm hot,
burned inside,
flipped over, roasted
and sprayed with oil.
Found a new fling.
He's got a match.
Now, I'm on fire.
He's hot.
Now, I'm melting down to the core.
I lower my sunglasses,
"Hi."
Yes, it's me,
A crazy, freaky, delirious, demented, and cracked

edition of your sweet, innocent friend.

I am crumbling,

loosening my screws,

I am cuckoo

for skin grabbing, hair pulling, lip squeezing, and finger biting.

Get me a straitjacket.

IN BETWEEN

In between

Lovers

Friends

In between

Sheets

Parked cars

In between

You

Me

In between

Our lips

Our hips

In between

Uncommitted

Exclusivity

In between

IN BETWEEN

QUICKSAND

Like quicksand you sucked me down
quickly, quietly, and seductively:
A hypnotic relation.
The ship of salvation never sailed in our seas.

You grabbed me with your stare
on the secluded beach.
Under the blackest sky-
Sparkling
Bling* bling*

We sink into the wettest sand,
you pulling my hair,
twisting it around your fingers
as we drop
down,
down,
down
pressed under the curl of a wave.
Salt on my lips
tingles my sunburned mouth.

Foamy sea rushing

in and out,

smoothing out the roughest stones.

Crystal blues and diamond foam

numbing toes and make us

say AHHH and OHH

IN MY ROBE

You don't listen to me,
but you listen to my sex.
I wear a robe of language
and you need a translator.
I'm soaked in the letters.
The words I feel for you
are like a seaweed body wrap
of love letters,
romantic prose,
passionate arguments,
and angry notes.
Unfortunately you don't read,
but see only invisible ink.
In your eyes, I am always naked.
I am a silent black and white movie
dancing around your bed.
I tell you the juiciest secrets
that you swallow like a shark does small fish.
Too blind to see this shimmery mermaid
staring at you lustfully.

TRIBAL

There's something naked about

dancing in the dark.

My arms do a wave,

then sway from side to side

like a cat on a tight rope.

Bass cuts the air

making pockets of space

to bounce in.

It's an animalistic sense.

I can smell your scent as you close in on me when the

circuits are closed.

I shake

..fast..

I am a part of a modern day tribe who've been lost,

trapped in time,

deep in the jungle for centuries,

shrinking heads and sacrificing animals.

A bright flash of light turns this dance floor

into a sacred dance space

around a blazing fire pit.

I spin and tumble, circling around its center.

Touching myself,
rocking my wavy locks,
I rub neon paint all over my chest
to the downbeat
as I glow in the strobe lights
that strike these walls
like lightning from meddling gods.

YOU MELODICALLY unwrap the sheets we've enveloped ourselves in, as we rolled through these pages, climaxed, and have now begun to button up this sensuous journey. This room exudes a serene darkness with its deep, ocean blue glow. I pull away from our intimacy finding a worldly picture and think of myself at a distance observing a mysterious pair of creatures. There, I see you and I lying together in bed. My appearance is that of a wild, jungle woman who's coming down off a high of fleshy pleasures. I breathe peacefully and slow. My heart finds a restful beat. Alleviated, I am on my stomach with my hand on your chest, in nothing but my nude pumps, stroking the space between your pecks. I wonder if you believe you've seen it all– every last part of me– through all the tangling, untangling, posing, pressing, and squeezing. We laugh at the idea of any deep connections between you and I at the bottom of these shallow sheets, but there is no time machine that could help us to see which way this erotic story may turn next.

We can only imagine what could be, as we continue to live out our passionate reveries. When you go, I'll continue to hold your scent, fantasizing about our next encounter–our next carnal rendezvous. I study your scars, your tattoos, your indentations, the creases in your skin, and every other unique mark. I've seen others like you. I've seen them come....and then go, but there is something inside me that loudly says *slow.slow...STOP!*

You get up to leave. I watch you stand, with your back turned to me. You adjust your belt on your smooth, sexy waist. Like a cat, I creep quietly to my bare feet. Slipping my arms over your shoulders, I put my hands on your chest, kiss the back of your neck, just as you like it, and you fall back into bed.

C.E. Zachary has a masters degree in English from Saint John's University. She teaches English as a Second Language in a New York City public school. *Reckless,* is her Second published volume of poetry. Stay tuned for more!

For more information about C.E. Zachary and her writing visit www.corinnez.blogspot.com and www.dreamwritenow.com.

Books by C. E. Zachary, *Like a Fairy in Love* and *Reckless,* are currently available on Amazon.com.

Made in the USA
Charleston, SC
06 July 2012